The Kids Laugh Challenge

Would You Rather?

Christmas Edition

Funny Scenarios, Wacky Choices and Hilarious Situations for Kids and Family

With Fun Illustrations

RIDDLELAND

Designs from Freepik.com

Table of Contents

Bonus Book!

RIDDLELAND

https://pixelfy.me/riddlelandbonus

Thank you for buying this book. We would like to share a special bonus as a token of appreciation. It is a collection of 50 original jokes, riddles, and two super funny stories!

Introduction

"May you never be too grown up to search the skies on Christmas Eve." ~ **Unknown**

We would like to personally thank you for purchasing this book. ***Would You Rather? Christmas Edition*** is a collection of the funniest scenarios, wacky choices, and hilarious situations for kids and adults to choose from.

These questions are an excellent way to get a conversation started in a fun and exciting way. Also, by asking "Why?" after a "Would you rather" question, you may find interesting answers and learn a lot about a person.

We wrote this book because we want children to be encouraged to read more, think, and grow. As parents, we know that when children play games and learn, they are being educated while having so much fun that they don't even realize they're learning and developing valuable life skills. 'Would you Rather ...' is one of our favorite games to play as a family. Some of the 'would you rather ...' scenarios have had us in fits of giggles, others have generated reactions such as: "Eeeeeeuuugh, that's gross!" and yet others still really make us think and reflect and consider our decisions.

Besides having fun, playing the game also has other benefits such as:

- **Communication** - This game helps children to interact, read aloud, and listen to others. It's a great way to connect. It's a fun way for parents to get their children interacting with them without a formal, awkward conversation. The game can also help to get to know someone better and learn about their likes, dislikes, and values.

- **Builds Confidence** - Children get used to pronouncing vocabulary, asking questions and it helps to deal with shyness.

- **Develops Critical Thinking** - It helps children to defend and justify the rationale for their choices and can generate discussions and debates. Parents playing this game with young children can give them prompting questions about their answers to help them reach logical and sensible decisions.

- **Improves Vocabulary** - Children will be introduced to new words in the questions, and the context of them will help them remember them because the game is fun.

- **Encourages Equality and Diversity** - Considering other people's answers, even if they differ from your own, is important for respect, equality, diversity, tolerance, acceptance, and inclusivity. Some questions may get children to think about options available to them, that don't fall into gendered stereotypes, i.e., careers or activities that challenge the norm.

Welcome to the Kids Laugh Challenge

Would You Rather?

Christmas Edition

How do you play?

At least two players are needed to play this game. Face your opponent and decide who is **Santa Elf 1** and **Santa Elf 2**. If you have 3 or 4 players, you can decide which players belong to **Santa Helpers 1** and **Santa Helpers 2**. The goal of the game is to score points by making the other players laugh. The first player to a score 10 points is the **Round Champion.**

What are the rules?

Santa Elf 1 starts first. Read the questions aloud and choose an answer. The same player will then explain why they chose the answer in the silliest and wackiest way possible. If the reason makes Santa Elf 2 laugh, then Santa Elf 1 scores a funny point. Take turns going back and forth and write down the score.

How do you get started?

Flip a coin. The Santa Elf that guesses it correctly starts first.

Bonus Tip: Making funny voices, silly dance moves or wacky facial expression will make your opponent laugh!

Most Importantly: Remember to have fun and enjoy the game!

Would You Rather...

Have a grumpy little pet gingerbread cookie named Ginger you absolutely can't eat OR a rather large red and white striped candy cane growing out of your nose?

Take a family photo wearing the ugliest Christmas sweater ever OR take a really fancy family photo where a big piece of hair is sticking out of your head in a wonky way but everyone else looks fabulous?

Would You Rather...

Be a snowman with a carrot nose that a reindeer keeps trying to eat OR have a pet reindeer in your backyard that you have to pooper scoop every day?

Have to make all new handmade ornaments for your Christmas tree every year OR cut strings of paper snowflake garland to cover your whole house?

Would You Rather...

Be followed to school by a super creepy group of really tiny snowmen OR find a very quiet and very large snowman hiding in your closet after school?

Have a giant blow up Santa Elf in your front yard who follows you with his eyes OR a giant blowup Rudolph outside your window whose red nose blinks through your bedroom window all night long?

Would You Rather...

Try to play in the snow with hands so hot that they melt the snow on contact OR have hands so cold that you need to wear mittens year-round?

Have an enormous hot pink Christmas tree in the middle of your living room OR wear a hot pink Santa suit to school for one day?

Would You Rather...

Only be able to eat snow for one whole day OR only be able to suck on icicles for one whole day?

Have to give away one of your belongings for every present you receive on Christmas OR get to buy a new item of your choice for someone else for every present you receive on Christmas?

Would You Rather...

Have a lovable pet snowman who needs to be rebuilt every day OR a pet abominable snowman who chews on your pillow?

Open presents sitting next to a Christmas tree that plays music and has lights that blink in rhythm OR have all the lights on your Christmas tree burn out right before you open presents?

Would You Rather...

Get hit in the face with a snowball every time you don't know the answer to a question on your homework OR get hit in the face with a snowball every time you tell a lie?

Go to bed on a soft pillow that smells like a pine tree is in your nose OR sleep on a bundle of real poky pine tree branches?

Would You Rather...

Be turned into a snowman and cursed to spend the rest of winter outside until you melt into a puddle OR have long icicles at the ends of your fingers instead of fingernails?

Get a ride to school in the back of Santa's supersonic sleigh OR ride to school on the back of a flying reindeer who smells like the back of an old barn?

Would You Rather...

Be adopted by a family of snowmen and live in a freezing cold house made of ice OR have a pet coconut named "Coco" who goes with you everywhere and has her very own little winter coat?

Have your teacher wear a Santa Claus suit to school every day in December OR grow a white fluffy beard like Santa Claus that you have to shave every day in December?

Would You Rather...

Build a snowman using dirty brown snow OR using bunny poops for the eyes on your snowman's face?

Try to make a creamy smoothie using hot chocolate and ice cubes OR make a yummy banana and yellow snow smoothie?

Would You Rather...

Be able to shake beautifully patterned snowflakes from your hair OR spit perfectly round little snowballs out of your mouth?

Get pulled to school on a sled by your dad OR go ice skating holding hands with your mom?

Would You Rather...

Wear a hat that is two sizes too big and is always falling over your eyes OR wear a pair of mismatched gloves, one that is too small and squishes your hand and one that is too big and keeps falling off?

Do the polar plunge where you dive into a cold lake or river in your swimsuit OR get a big bear hug from someone who just did the polar plunge into a cold lake or river?

Would You Rather...

Wear gloves that stick to everything you touch outside OR wear mittens that make your arms feel heavy because they're super soggy and wet?

Spend your day chopping wood with an axe for an old-fashioned fireplace OR weaving an evergreen wreath for your front door?

Would You Rather...

Go outside with wet hair that freezes stiff in the cold and breaks off when the wind blows OR shave your head bald and never wear a hat in the winter?

Eat a bowlful of marshmallows that have hard and crunchy pieces of candy cane in them OR eat a handful of candy canes that are squishy like fresh marshmallows?

Would You Rather...

Wear a knitted scarf that smells like cinnamon wrapped tightly around your face OR wear a soggy scarf wrapped tightly around your face?

Ride to school on a chilly school bus that doesn't have a working heater OR walk to school on a really icy slippery sidewalk?

Would You Rather...

Try to make 100 paper snowflakes with a pair of old rusty scissors OR try to make 100 snowflakes using old cereal boxes instead of paper?

Get chased around the playground all day by a gingerbread cookie come to life OR bake the most amazing looking gingerbread cookie that smells like rotten milk?

Would You Rather...

Spend a whole day catching snowflakes and looking at them under a microscope OR stay outside all day during a blizzard trying to measure the snowfall with a ruler?

Spend Christmas Eve with your family singing Christmas carols outside around your whole neighborhood OR at the shopping mall wrapping presents for other people?

Would You Rather...

Use a really tipsy ladder to put the head on top of your very tall snowman OR have a giant chunk of ice fall off your roof and hit you hard in the head?

Build a snowman on a cold day using only your hands OR shovel your driveway clean using only a dinner spoon?

Would You Rather...

Be able to freeze things by touching them with your fingers OR leave slushy footprints wherever you walk?

Go sledding while wearing nothing on your bare feet OR have a fruitcake fight while wearing a pair of stinky socks on your hands?

Would You Rather...

Walk around with two giant blocks of ice instead of feet OR try to get through a school day with hands so frozen that you can't move your fingers?

Spend the day digging tunnels through giant snow hills like an ant in an ant farm OR get lost in the tunnels you've dug and have to spend the night inside them?

Would You Rather...

Play outside at recess in a blizzard where you can't see anything OR have to stay inside at your desk with your head down instead?

Hibernate (sleep) all winter long like a grizzly bear OR walk to school through deep snow drifts every day all winter long?

Would You Rather...

Wear a pair of gloves on the wrong hands OR wear your boots on the wrong feet for a whole week?

Get so cold outside that your skin turns bright red and stays that way all day OR get so cold outside that your lips turn deep blue and stay that way all day?

Would You Rather...

Be a papa penguin spending all of your time with an egg between your feet waiting for it to hatch OR have snowshoes super glued to your feet so you can never take them off?

Have a giant stack of Christmas presents under a really sad and spindly Christmas tree OR only get one Christmas present under a beautiful big evergreen Christmas tree?

Would You Rather...

Grow pine tree scented hair out of your ears OR grow spiky pine needles instead of hair?

Open your Christmas presents with one hand tied behind your back OR open your Christmas presents using only your feet?

Would You Rather...

Live in a really hot country where it never ever snows OR a country with so much snow that your school is actually made out of snow?

Be transformed into Santa Claus with a large belly and white beard, and his red and white outfit until Christmas Day? OR be transformed into one of Santa's Elves working at his toy factory until Christmas Eve?

Would You Rather...

Wear a pair of white socks that are now a dirty brown on your hands as mittens OR a pair of wet and smelly mittens on your feet instead of socks?

Celebrate Christmas in a place with lots of sun and palm trees OR in a place with beautiful winter snowflakes and shovels?

Would You Rather...

Wear a winter hat that makes your head super itchy OR a pair of snow pants that are too tight around the waist so you have to suck in your stomach?

Eat a fruitcake sandwich - two pieces of fruitcake with a sugar cookie in between OR drink a peppermint, hot chocolate, and eggnog milkshake?

Would You Rather...

Skate at a turtle's crawling speed using super dull ice skates OR ski frighteningly fast down a hill on butter-coated skis?

Be the forgotten tenth reindeer who is left out of all the Christmas stories OR be the dog who has to pull the Grinch's sleigh in Dr. Seuss's *How the Grinch Stole Christmas!?*

Would You Rather...

Have a snowball fight using scoops of ice cream OR a water gun fight using hot chocolate?

Eat a stack of pancakes drizzled with eggnog OR eat a candy cane dipped in maple syrup?

Would You Rather...

Burn your tongue on a smoking hot cup of hot chocolate OR take an ice-cold shower because your brother or sister used up all of the hot water?

Take a vacation to a really cool place for Christmas but have to spend two days at airports to get there and back OR stay home and be bored in your pajamas all day long on Christmas?

Would You Rather...

Find a dead bug floating in your cup of hot chocolate OR drink a cup of hot chocolate that someone dumped a bottle of cinnamon into?

Open Christmas presents with your large family going in order from oldest to youngest OR find that your cat has already tore into all your Christmas presents?

Would You Rather...

Drink a cup of hot chocolate after your dog just slurped out of it OR sit on a chair covered in freshly spilled hot chocolate?

Spend two whole days shopping for Christmas presents with your mom but get everything you want for Christmas OR spend two days playing in the snow instead and not get a single present that you like?

Would You Rather...

Write a letter to Santa using a squeezy bottle of ketchup OR by squeezing pickle juice from a big dill pickle?

Have Frosty the Snowman as your gym teacher so gym class is outside all winter long OR play in gym class all winter long wearing your snow boots instead of sneakers?

Would You Rather...

Get missed by Santa Claus because you are on vacation at Christmastime OR get the same exact present from Santa every single year of your life?

Eat a piece of fruitcake every meal for an entire week OR sleep on a block of hard fruitcake instead of a pillow for a week?

Would You Rather...

Glue a bunch of cotton balls to your face like Santa's beard OR spend a day rolling around in a giant plastic ornament like you're in a hamster ball?

Wear cheesy matching Christmas pajamas with your family OR grow a big fuzzy pair of reindeer antlers out of your ears?

Would You Rather...

Be naughty and risk getting no presents from Santa OR be the kid nobody likes because you're always telling them they'll end up on the naughty list?

Use $150 to buy the perfect presents for your entire family OR to buy something that you've really been wanting for yourself?

Would You Rather...

Be Santa Claus and get the joy of delivering Christmas presents to children for Christmas OR be Mrs. Claus and get the joy of keeping Santa Claus fat all year by feeding him cookies?

Live in a house made from yummy frosted gingerbread OR inside of a house made out of creamy cold peppermint chocolate chip ice cream?

Would You Rather...

Grow a big large white fluffy beard like Santa Claus OR have a big jiggly jelly belly like Santa Claus?

Wake up and find coal in your stocking but cool toys in your siblings' stockings OR find pairs of socks and underwear in your stocking on Christmas morning?

Would You Rather...

Wake up Christmas morning to find out that your stocking has disappeared and there are no presents from Santa for you OR find a bunch of school supplies from Santa in your stocking?

Get the least number of presents in your whole family on Christmas morning OR get a whole pile of really tiny little presents under the tree?

Would You Rather...

Have a nose that blinks red like Rudolph the Red Nosed Reindeer's every time you tell a lie OR have a really loud and annoying alarm go off every time you do something that puts you on the naughty list?

Spend a whole afternoon replacing burned out Christmas bulbs on ten strings of lights OR spend a whole evening driving around in the car with your family looking at lame Christmas light displays?

Would You Rather...

Believe that you are one of Santa's workshop elves and make everyone call you "Woody" OR believe that you are a toy brought to life by Santa's magic and make everyone call you "Buddy"?

Get picked to sing a solo in your school's Christmas concert but have stage fright OR sing the solo confidently until you embarrassingly blank out and forget the words to the song?

Would You Rather...

Have your hair turn snowy white like Santa's OR find yourself saying "ho ho ho, Merry Christmas" fifty times a day?

Have a family who takes "silent night" very seriously so you can't talk at all on Christmas Eve OR have a family who spends all night on Christmas Eve singing Christmas carols?

Would You Rather...

Grow big fluffy white Santa beards coming out of your armpits OR one big white fluffy Santa beard coming out of your belly button?

Break a tooth eating a piece of your grandma's fruitcake OR suffer a serious injury from the tape dispenser while wrapping Christmas presents?

Would You Rather...

Accidentally eat the last Christmas cookie before Christmas Eve so you have none to leave for Santa OR accidentally eat half of the last cookie and leave the bitten off part sitting on a plate for Santa along with an apology note?

Sleep in a bed filled with crumbled sugar cookie crumbs OR stick to your bed sheets because you are covered with gooey candy cane syrup?

Would You Rather...

Be forced by your parents to go to the shopping mall and take a picture with Santa Claus OR be forced to dress up like a candy cane for the annual Christmas play?

Go Christmas shopping one hour a day for the whole month of December OR read the same Christmas book before bed every night for the whole month of December?

Would You Rather...

Have a Christmas tree made only of chewed bubble gum ornaments OR candy canes that have already been sucked on?

Listen to a bunch of out-of-tune Christmas carolers for two hours OR watch a two-hour long Christmas movie in a language that you don't understand?

Would You Rather...

Have five strings of Christmas lights wrapped tightly around your whole body OR crawl around on the floor underneath your Christmas tree picking up every single fallen needle?

Secretly unwrap and rewrap all of your presents before Christmas so you know what everything is OR secretly trade name tags with one of your sibling's presents that you really want?

Would You Rather...

Sneeze every time you are around a Christmas tree OR break out with big red itchy bumps every time you touch snow?

Spend twenty-four hours watching the same Christmas show on repeat OR sit in front of the TV for as long as it takes to watch every Christmas show ever made?

Would You Rather...

Have the same annoying Christmas carol stuck in your head for a whole week OR not be able to stop singing that same annoying Christmas carol nonstop for a whole day?

Spend an entire day walking around covered in Christmas lights from head to toe OR go to sleep in a bedroom that has 2,000 Christmas lights strung from the ceiling and walls?

Would You Rather...

End every sentence with "fa-la-la" OR begin every sentence with "ho-ho-ho" in the month of December?

Wake up every morning to your little brother or sister dipping your finger into a cup of warm hot chocolate OR wake up every morning to your little brother or sister dumping a bucket of cold snow onto your face?

Would You Rather...

Spend one hour straight licking Christmas card envelopes OR lick one envelope and get a huge papercut on your tongue?

Dance in a fluffy tutu for The Nutcracker ballet OR go house to house in your neighborhood singing Christmas carols?

Would You Rather...

Say "goody goody gumdrops" every time someone tells you a joke OR laugh with a hearty "ho ho ho"?

Build a gingerbread house using chewed bubble gum to "glue" it together OR eat a gingerbread house made from your dog's biscuits?

Would You Rather...

Open a bunch of Christmas presents covered with a ridiculous amount of sticky tape OR presents that have been wrapped using rolls and rolls of toilet paper?

Live in the North Pole where there's no Wi-Fi or TV OR be stranded on a tropical island with a cell phone that has 5% battery?

Would You Rather...

Have a Christmas with no presents under the tree OR an Easter with no candy in your Easter basket?

Get your most wished-for Christmas present and find out it is broken and the stores are all closed so you can't return it OR get a really ugly homemade Christmas sweater from your aunt that you have to wear all day long?

Would You Rather...

Wear a sweater with jingle bells that tinkle wherever you go OR wear a pair of striped elf pants, pointy elf shoes, and a tall floppy hat?

Eat a giant stack of sugar cookies drenched in maple syrup for Christmas Day breakfast OR a bunch of cardboard cookies covered with super sweet frosting?

Would You Rather...

Spend twenty-four hours wrapped inside of a giant Christmas present OR spend twenty-four hours carrying around a backpack filled with really heavy Christmas presents?

Celebrate Christmas with lots of presents except everyone is super crabby OR celebrate a Christmas with only one present where everyone is super chilled and happy?

Would You Rather...

Have your mom post a really embarrassing picture of you in your pjs on Christmas morning OR accidentally break the special Christmas present you made at school for your parents before you get to give it to them?

Have an all-out snowball fight with your friends using only your left hand OR ice skate for an hour balancing only on your left foot?

Would You Rather...

Accidentally break your mom's favorite Christmas ornament while decorating the tree OR watch your little brother or sister step on your favorite ornament on purpose?

Eat a handful of bright yellow snow from your backyard OR roll around in a pile of yellow snow wearing only your underpants?

Would You Rather...

Have red and white candy cane stripes all over your body OR a coating of gumdrop sugar that you can't wash off of your body?

Have to share a bed with your little brother or sister because you gave your room to Grandma and Grandpa while they stay for Christmas OR have to sleep on the couch with your dog snoring loudly on the floor?

Would You Rather...

Eat a bowl of minty candy cane flavored oatmeal for breakfast OR take a bath in a giant tub of thick creamy eggnog?

Have all Santa's reindeers as your housekeepers OR live with Santa in the North pole 364 days a year?

Would You Rather...

Have a red-light bulb on your head that lights up when you don't know the answer to a question OR have a green light bulb on your head that lights up when you do know the answer to a question?

Sit in a steamy warm outdoor hot tub on a really cold day OR take a long winter's nap in a cozy little snow cave?

Would You Rather...

Eat a dozen unfrosted and tasteless sugar cookies OR eat a dozen candy canes that have no peppermint flavor at all?

Play a game of basketball wearing a pair of thick and fuzzy mittens OR play volleyball barefoot in the snow?

Would You Rather...

Have hard little reindeer hooves for feet that make it impossible to sneak up on anyone OR wear super big and pointy elf shoes on your feet that you keep tripping over?

Be snowed in at school overnight with your teacher and classmates OR get snowed out of a week of school but then have to go to school one week extra in the summer?

Would You Rather...

Eat a dozen sugar cookies frosted with mustard and ketchup OR suck on a pickle flavored candy cane?

Use a very poky pine branch to scratch a pesky itch on your back OR a candy cane as a spoon to try to eat your breakfast cereal?

Would You Rather...

Open all your presents like a crazy person in less than five minutes at Christmas OR spend five very long and slow hours opening presents with your family?

Spend your recess helping sweaty little kids get their smelly snow gear on OR playing freeze tag with your friends on a really cold day?

Would You Rather...

Begin every meal by eating a super minty candy cane OR by drinking a giant glass of creamy eggnog?

Play on a playground that is covered with little round frozen rabbit poops OR one that is covered with patches of yellow snow?

Would You Rather...

Be Santa Claus and get stuck inside of a chimney because you ate too many sugar cookies OR turn black from head to toe because of all the coal in the chimneys you slid down?

Wear a red and black checkered flannel shirt that smells like a sweaty man OR wear a hockey player's unwashed gear for the whole winter?

Would You Rather...

Wear a red and white furry Santa suit, complete with a big white beard, to the beach on a hot day OR go outside during a blizzard wearing nothing but your swimsuit?

Soak your socks on the slushy playground and have to wear someone else's socks from the lost and found OR soak your pants and have to wear someone else's pants from the lost and found?

Would You Rather...

Open a bunch of beautifully wrapped presents that have nothing in them OR get two awesome presents that look like they've been run over by Santa's sleigh?

Write a letter to Santa as a school project, rewriting it twenty times until your teacher says it's perfect OR write a quick letter to Santa misspelling the items on your list and getting the wrong things?

Would You Rather...

Drink a cup of hot chocolate while sitting on a warm sunny beach OR drink a cup of ice-cold lemonade while standing in the middle of a big white snowbank?

Drink a gingerbread cookie eggnog smoothie OR eat a gingerbread cookie that is frosted with eggnog icing?

Would You Rather...

Make a sled out of cardboard and spend an afternoon using it at the sledding hill OR make a pair of ice skates using old shoes with butter knives attached and spend an afternoon at the skating rink?

Put a pinch of yellow snow in your hot chocolate to cool it off OR drink a cup of hot chocolate with rock hard marshmallows floating all over it?

Would You Rather...

Play hide and seek by completely burying yourself in snowbanks OR play a game of high-speed tag on the ice-skating rink?

Fall off your sled and tumble in a bunch of somersaults all the way down the rest of the hill OR climb all the way to the top of a big sledding hill and accidentally drop your sled so it slides down without you on it?

Would You Rather...

Play in sticky snow that sticks all over your whole body like glue OR try to build a snowman with snow that melts the instant that you touch it?

Ride down a hill on the back of a sled where you can't see anything in front of you OR ride on a sled tied to another sled so you can't control exactly where your sled is going?

Would You Rather...

Have the body of a big misshapen lumpy snowman OR the skinny twiggy arms of a snowman that has no feet?

Know if you are on Santa's naughty list so you can improve your behavior OR always believe you are on Santa's good list even though you sometimes aren't?

Would You Rather...

Spend your day ice fishing through a tiny hole in the ice not catching any fish OR spend your day walking through the woods looking for a tree that you can cut down?

Spend three hours waiting in line with your little brother or sister to see Santa Claus at the shopping mall OR wait in line to see Santa for two hours and then he has an emergency at the North Pole and has to leave for the day before you get to see him?

Would You Rather...

Have big fist-sized holes in the armpits of your winter jacket OR lots of tiny holes in the thumbs of each of your mittens?

Dress up as an elf with your siblings and your parents as Mr. and Mrs. Claus for your annual family photo OR have your faces put onto the bodies of Santa's reindeer for the annual family photo?

Would You Rather...

Be able to shoot snowballs out of your belly button OR have pine tree scented armpits?

Try to cut wrapping paper for your presents using your fingers instead of scissors OR wrap all your Christmas presents using chewed bubble gum instead of scotch tape?

Would You Rather...

Wear a big fluffy hat made from fake rabbit fur to school OR a warm knitted hat that has two very large jingle bells on top of it instead of a puff ball?

Eat a stale old gingerbread house leftover from Christmas five years ago OR eat a fruitcake from the year that you were born?

Would You Rather...

Wear winter scarves tied around your feet instead of snow boots OR wear snow boots on your hands instead of mittens?

Help out packing Christmas presents for a Shoe box appeal before Christmas OR help out collecting food to give to a food bank before Christmas?

Would You Rather...

Try to write out your homework using a pencil while wearing a pair of really puffy mittens OR try to run a fast mile in gym class while wearing your overall snow pants?

Sit at a school desk which is covered in bright cheerful Christmas lights OR use a chunk of coal instead of a pencil to do your homework?

Would You Rather...

Wear a winter jacket with a sticky zipper which is super hard to unzip OR one size too big snow boots that are always falling off when you're walking through the snow?

Spend every day of your Christmas vacation shoveling snow from the sidewalks OR spend every day of your Christmas vacation stuck in the house because you are snowed in?

Would You Rather...

Play a game of ice hockey using a frozen doughnut instead of a puck OR have a snowball fight using frozen cupcakes?

Wake up in the middle of the night to discover Santa Claus delivering your presents OR to discover your Elf on a Shelf moving to a new hiding spot?

Would You Rather...

Wear a backpack to school that has been stuffed full of fluffy snow OR wear a pair of boots that are filled with slushy snow?

Sleep underneath your Christmas tree to protect your presents the whole month of December OR have one of your presents disappear every day for one week?

Would You Rather...

Live on a tropical island where it only snows one day a year OR in an Artic place where there is only one day a year that it doesn't snow?

Take home a real Christmas tree that has a sleeping squirrel inside of it OR take home a Christmas tree that drops all its needles on your floor overnight?

Would You Rather...

Have a sword fight using giant icicles from your rooftop OR splash in slushy snow puddles?

Have the friendly and magical Frosty the Snowman for your teacher but not be able to use the classroom heater or he'll melt OR have Santa Claus who is so busy at the North Pole that he usually has a substitute teacher in class for him?

Would You Rather...

Have to wear your big brother or sister's dirty and holey winter hand me downs OR wear last year's snow pants that are so short they barely go below your knees?

Spend your afternoon pulling kids on their sleds up to the top of a snow hill OR work as a skate monitor watching kids ice skate at the rink?

Would You Rather...

Turn completely white in the wintertime to camouflage your body with the white snow OR turn completely green in the summertime to camouflage your body with the green grass?

Drink a hot cup of really watery hot chocolate OR a too-chocolatey cup of way too cool hot chocolate?

Would You Rather...

Break your leg by slipping on a patch of black ice and wear a cast all winter OR get your tongue stuck to a metal fence pole and wear a bandage on it for two days?

Stick your tongue to a metal slide on the playground OR have a bunch of snow stuffed down the back of your snow pants?

Would You Rather...

Faceplant into a big fluffy snowbank OR step onto a frozen puddle and your foot breaks through into ice cold water?

Go outside during a snowstorm of paper snowflakes that give you a bunch of little, yet painful, papercuts OR spend an hour pretending to play in a pile of fake snow for your family pictures?

Would You Rather...

Buy a package of candy canes and find that every single one is broken OR buy a dozen gingerbread men and find that someone bit off every single head?

Spend five hours building a giant snow fort that completely melts in one day OR build a super strong large snow fort that you and your family move into?

Would You Rather...

Hold the world record for making the most paper snowflakes in twenty-four hours OR the world record for making the largest paper snowflake, one bigger than your house?

Spend all day trying to build a snow fort with snow that just crumbles apart OR spend all day trying to build a sandcastle with dry sand that won't stick together?

Would You Rather...

Carve really amazing ice sculptures that always melt within a day OR create amazing sand sculptures that get washed away by the tide every evening?

Play a game of baseball using snowballs instead of baseballs OR play a game of dodgeball using snowballs instead of rubber balls?

Would You Rather...

Eat a bowl of Christmas tree flavored ice cream OR have a Christmas tree that smells like peppermint candy canes instead of pine?

Get stuck in a blizzard where the electricity goes out and you have no TV or video games OR be in a blizzard where your furnace goes out so there is no heat and you have to wear all of your winter gear inside?

Would You Rather...

Skateboard on a really slippery ice-skating rink OR play hockey while wearing a pair of roller skates?

Play soccer in the snow with a rock-hard frozen soccer ball OR try to play volleyball using a beach ball on a really windy day?

Would You Rather...

Never be able to get in the Christmas mood and say "bah hambug" all of the time Or walk around singing "Joy to the World" to everyone you meet?

Have your foot stomped on by one of Santa's reindeer OR run over by the runners on Santa's sleigh?

Would You Rather...

Spend a night outside in the snow with only your survival skills to build a fire and stay warm OR accidentally get left home by yourself when your family leaves for Christmas vacation?

Take care of Santa's reindeers by brushing them, feeding them, and pooper scooping their stalls OR be the cook in charge of feeding all of Santa's elves at the workshop, some of whom are very picky eaters?

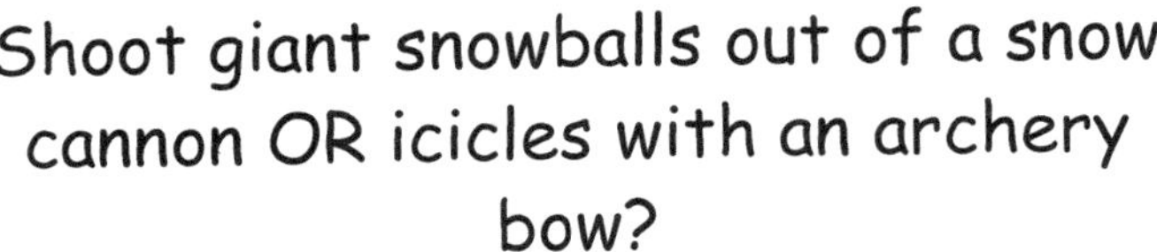

Shoot giant snowballs out of a snow cannon OR icicles with an archery bow?

Have a giant blowup Christmas tree in your living room instead of a real tree OR live with really grinchy parents who don't ever get in the Christmas spirit?

Would You Rather...

Sled down a giant snow hill wearing a blindfold OR try to play a game of ice hockey with the stick duct taped to your hands?

Pull your friends around the playground on a big sled like Santa's reindeer OR work at the North Pole shoveling reindeer poo for Santa Claus?

Would You Rather...

Find a bushy squirrel living in one of your snow boots OR a tiny little mouse cuddled up in the thumb of your mitten?

Forget to water your Christmas tree so all its needles fall off before Christmas OR overwater your Christmas tree until it gets a really funky smell to it?

Would You Rather...

Step on a broken Christmas ornament and hurt your foot OR trip into your Christmas tree and break a whole bunch of ornaments but not hurt yourself?

Have to hand-draw every Christmas card that you send to all your classmates OR instead of sending Christmas cards donate money to a charity?

If you did, we are ecstatic. If not, please write your complaint to us and we will make ensure to fix it.

If you're feeling generous, there is something important that you can help me with - tell other people that you enjoyed the book.

Ask a grown-up to write about it on Amazon. When they do, more people will find out about the book. It also lets Amazon know that we are making kids around the world laugh. Even a few words and ratings would go a long way.

If you have any ideas or jokes that you think are super funny, please let us know. We would love to hear from you. Our email address is - **riddleland@riddlelandforkids.com**

Bonus Book!

RIDDLELAND

https://pixelfy.me/riddlelandbonus

Thank you for buying this book. As a token of our appreciation, we would like to offer a special bonus—a collection of 50 original jokes, riddles, and funny stories.

Would you like your jokes and riddles to be featured in our next book?

We are having a contest to see who are the smartest or funniest boys and girls in the world! :

1) **Creative and Challenging Riddles**
2) **Tickle Your Funny Bone Contest**

Parents, please email us your child's "original" riddle or joke and **he or she could win a $50 Amazon gift card and be featured in our next book.**

Here are the rules:

1) It must be challenging for the riddles and funny for the jokes!
2) It must be 100% Original and not something from the Internet! It is easy to find out!
3) You can submit both jokes and riddles as they are 2 separate contests.
4) No help from the parents unless they are as funny as you.
5) Winners will be announced via email or our Facebook group - Riddleland for kids
6) Please also mention what book you purchased.
7) Email us at Riddleland@riddlelandforkids.com

Other Fun Books By Riddleland

Riddles Series

FUN RIDDLES AND TRICK QUESTIONS FOR KIDS AND FAMILY!
300 RIDDLES AND BRAIN TEASERS THAT KIDS AND FAMILY WILL ENJOY
RIDDLELAND

CREATIVE RIDDLES AND TRICK QUESTIONS FOR KIDS AND FAMILY!
300 RIDDLES AND BRAIN TEASERS THAT KIDS AND FAMILY WILL ENJOY
RIDDLELAND

FUN RIDDLES AND TRICK QUESTIONS FOR KIDS AND FAMILY
EASTER EDITION
HUNDREDS OF RIDDLES AND BRAIN TEASERS THAT KIDS AND FAMILY WILL ENJOY
RIDDLELAND

FUN RIDDLES AND TRICK QUESTIONS FOR KIDS AND FAMILY
ST PATRICK'S DAY EDITION
HUNDREDS OF RIDDLES AND BRAIN TEASERS THAT KIDS AND FAMILY WILL ENJOY
RIDDLELAND

WITH FUN! ILLUSTRATIONS
AWESOME RIDDLES AND TRICK QUESTIONS FOR KIDS
300 FUN BRAIN-STUMPERS FOR AGES 9 TO 12
RIDDLELAND

WITH FUN! ILLUSTRATIONS
AWESOME RIDDLES AND TRICK QUESTIONS FOR KIDS
PUZZLING QUESTIONS AND FUN FACTS FOR AGES 5 TO 8
RIDDLELAND

WITH FUN ILLUSTRATIONS!
FUN HALLOWEEN RIDDLES AND TRICK QUESTIONS FOR KIDS AND FAMILY!
300 RIDDLES AND BRAIN TEASERS THAT KIDS AND FAMILY WILL ENJOY
RIDDLELAND

WITH FUN ILLUSTRATIONS!
FUN THANKSGIVING RIDDLES AND TRICK QUESTIONS FOR KIDS AND FAMILY!
300 RIDDLES AND BRAIN TEASERS THAT KIDS AND FAMILY WILL ENJOY
RIDDLELAND

WITH FUN ILLUSTRATIONS
FUN CHRISTMAS RIDDLES AND TRICK QUESTIONS FOR KIDS AND FAMILY!
300 RIDDLES AND BRAIN TEASERS THAT KIDS AND FAMILY WILL ENJOY
RIDDLELAND

The Laugh Challenge Joke Series

Would You Rather Series

Get them on Amazon

or our website at www.riddlelandforkids.com

Riddleland is a mom + dad run publishing company. We are passionate about creating fun and innovative books to help children develop their reading skills and fall in love with reading. If you have suggestions for us or want to work with us, shoot us an email at riddleland@riddlelandforkids.com

Our family's favorite quote:

"Creativity is an area in which younger people have a tremendous advantage since they have an endearing habit of always questioning past wisdom and authority." - Bill Hewlett

CPSIA information can be obtained
at www.ICGtesting.com
Printed in the USA
LVHW081347281120
672917LV00036B/796

9 781951 592646